# silent witness

*How DNA Uncovered the Truth and Empowered My Healing*

## ashley spence

FREILING AGENCY

Copyright © 2024 by Ashley Spence
First Paperback Edition

All rights reserved. No part of this publication may be reproduced, distributed, or transmitted in any form or by any means, including photocopying, recording, or other electronic or mechanical methods, without the prior written permission of the publisher, except in the case of brief quotations embodied in critical reviews and certain other noncommercial uses permitted by copyright law. For permission requests, write to the publisher, addressed "Attention: Permissions Coordinator," at the address below.

Some names, businesses, places, events, locales, incidents, and identifying details inside this book have been changed to protect the privacy of individuals.

Published by Freiling Agency, LLC.

P.O. Box 1264
Warrenton, VA 20188

www.FreilingAgency.com

PB ISBN: 978-1-963701-29-6
E-book ISBN: 978-1-963701-30-2

# Contents

Foreword ................................................................. v
1  Innocence ........................................................... 1
2  Darkness ............................................................ 15
3  Intuition and Fate .............................................. 19
4  Tragedy ............................................................. 25
5  Fighter .............................................................. 43
6  Surrender .......................................................... 51
7  I Got the Call .................................................... 59
8  Wanderlust ........................................................ 69
9  Trial .................................................................. 79
10 Forgiveness and Healing ................................... 97
Epilogue ................................................................ 105
Afterword – Sexual Healing ................................... 111

# Foreword

"Look, Mama! A butterfly!"

My daughter's voice bursts with excitement. We're running along the Town Lake Trail in Austin, chasing after my son on his bike. A butterfly glides past, leading the way before it flutters over the water. The sunlight dances on the surface, leaving behind shimmering reflections. "Yes, sweet girl," I say, smiling at her. "That's an angel from heaven, reminding us she's with us."

AUSTIN'S TOWN LAKE Trail holds a special place in my heart. It's where I go to make sense of life's most painful moments. When I faced loss, or when I didn't make the high school basketball "A Team," the trail became my refuge—a place to cry, to grieve, and to heal. It was here, years later, that I confronted the deep wounds left by a brutal home invasion I experienced in college. My tears fell alongside the path as I wrestled with anger and shame.

Even when my children were little, the trail called to us. After their father and I divorced, spending time outdoors felt like the best way to heal our hearts. Walking together on that trail gave us a sense of peace and togetherness. It reminded me that even in times of separation, we could still find ways to feel whole.

In my darkest moments, I would come here and pray, asking the heavens for a sign that everything would be okay. Without fail, a bright butterfly would appear, gently floating by. It was as if the Universe was telling me: You are heard. You are guided. You are not alone. Each time, I was reminded that transformation, though painful, is part of life's journey—a journey that strengthens our faith and leads us to the light.

Transformation is not easy. It's messy and uncomfortable, but it's also where we discover the beauty of resilience. It's where we learn to be gentle with ourselves, to get up after we fall, and to rebuild with a heart that shines brighter, stronger, and more compassionate than before.

We need to move our bodies, connect with nature, scream, cry, and speak up for ourselves and others. We need those pivotal moments—the conversations that challenge us, the people who appear in our lives at just the right time, the whispers of the Spirit that reminds us we're not alone. And we need to celebrate the victories, no matter how small they seem.

# Foreword

The Greek goddess Akeso is a powerful symbol of healing—she represents not the cure, but the journey itself. And isn't that what life is? One continuous process of healing, of uncovering truths, of contracting and expanding, falling and rising. It's hard. It's messy. It's emotional. And yes, it's lonely sometimes. But it's also full of joy, love, hope, and light. When we allow ourselves to face the darkness, we gain the strength to transform it into light.

My hope is that this book inspires you to begin—or continue—your own healing journey. If you're in the dark right now, look for the light, even if it's just a faint flicker. It's always there, guiding you back home. The caterpillar must struggle in its cocoon before it can become a butterfly. That struggle builds the strength and grace it needs to fly. This is my story, but it's not mine alone. It's a story shared by so many. I hope that, by reading it, you'll find your own path to healing—whatever that looks like for you.

You're worth it. Let's begin.

# 1

# Innocence

I WAS BLESSED with a childhood filled with joy, safety, and love.

My parents modeled a strong marriage. They loved and prioritized each other, and have been married now for almost fifty years. But they also prioritized me. For as long as I can remember, they were deeply involved in my life. My siblings and I were fortunate to be raised by people who treasured us and who instilled in us the values of selflessness, hard work, and generosity.

Above all, we knew what it meant to be deeply loved. I never questioned how much they loved me. My childhood was idyllic and just what every loving parent wants for their kids. We were shielded from life's harder edges and allowed to flourish into the best versions of ourselves.

My father, Roy Spence, was born in Brownwood, Texas. But his roots run deep in Eagle Pass—a small town on the Texas-Mexico border. There, they called him "Royito"—a nickname for "little Roy" since his father was known as "Big Roy." He loved his life growing up in Brownwood and has never forgotten where he came from. His mother was a school teacher and his father worked hard from being a car salesman, roofer, and builder to make ends meet. They didn't have much, but their love was abundant. My dad created his own world from the challenges he faced, and in doing so, helped others along the way.

He's an inspiration not just to me, but to so many who know him.

One of the stories from my dad's childhood that has always stuck with me is about my aunt, his sister. She had spina bifida. She wasn't able to walk. As a kid, my dad hated seeing her left out of the normal activities other children enjoyed. He pushed her to and from school every day. He and his friends would push her to the park and take her everywhere. He wanted her to feel a sense of belonging—to feel normal.

That sort of action-based love is the kind that changes lives. She lived decades longer than any doctor ever predicted, and I believe my father's love and commitment had a lot to do with that. When she passed away, my dad held her hand. He said that was the moment he realized, "All those years I thought I was pushing her, she was pushing me to live a life of purpose."

"You never know what someone else is going through," Dad would always say. He walked the talk, and made sure I did, too.

He attended the University of Texas in Austin after high school with dreams of becoming a lawyer. That's what his grandfather and uncle had done, and it seemed like a way to build the kind of career and life he dreamed about. He's even admitted to me that he dreamed of one day being the Governor of Texas!

But deep down, this was never the right fit for him.

He likes to tell the story of the day his LSAT scores came back. "Believe it or not," he says, "I didn't tell anyone I hated the law class. I started taking the LSAT test later on and never finished it. The University of Texas sent me a notice about the grade of the LSAT. I got it and threw it on the ground. True story: my dog actually tore it up. So I did not know what the letter said. My mom kept asking me how I did on the lawyers test. I told her I didn't know. She thought I had failed it. One day I finally told her the truth. And in fact, I did not know. The key point is that I thought if I took the test that I just might pass it. And if I passed it, I would then have to go to law school!"

That's my dad's style. He listens to his heart and makes bold decisions. At this point in his life, he had something much bigger than law school in mind. He'd met some people in college that he really liked, and they started an advertising agency in downtown Austin, in 1972, called GSD&M. They built brands, and they loved it. But for them, this venture was about a lot more than just business. It was about building purpose. My dad's mission was to inspire people to live their lives on purpose. He taught me, and countless others, that life is too short to be anything else but great at what you love. "Don't be mediocre at what you're bad at," he says. "Be great at what you're good at." His spirit was never mild. He even once marketed his own hot sauce company out of an Airstream trailer with the slogan: "Don't do mild."

Beyond business, Dad has always been about finding the good in life. He's the founder of The Purpose Institute, where he helps people discover their life's mission beyond just making a living. He launched the Make it Movement.org in his seventies with one goal: To use marketing as a force for good to inspire young Americans to find their career and purpose without needing to fit into the mold of a traditional four-year college education.

His entrepreneurial spirit didn't stop, even when most people normally start thinking about slowing down.

He also loves the outdoors. This shaped a big part of who I am today. I can remember many hours spent walking the Town Lake Trail with our black lab, Ellie. He even wrote a book about it—*Every Town Needs a Trail*. Ellie was his companion through life's ups and downs. I remember how much joy their time on that trail brought him. When Ellie died, the memories were so strong that the trail became bittersweet. But Dad doesn't stop. He decided to take his love for walking to the next level. He literally walked across America.

I joined him in Pennsylvania for part of this journey. By the time he got there, he had a scruffy gray beard. He had his camera in hand in order to photograph something he liked from every mile. His mission was never about the walk, but about the connections he made along the way.

My dad is an inspiration. He shows me, and many others, what it means to "walk your own road." I can't imagine how to live my own life without this lesson etched deep into my soul.

My mother is Mary. She comes from a large Lebanese family—our family reunions could easily fill a ballroom.

Her father owned grocery stores in Peoria, Illinois. Alongside my grandmother, he made many sacrifices to give my mother the life they couldn't have themselves. In turn, my mother dedicated her life to us. She was, and still is, our family's anchor.

In many ways, she's not like my dad. She's quieter. Her love runs deep and she's always focused on others, but she shares it privately and without fanfare. She prefers a quiet, face-to-face conversation over big crowds and lots of attention.

She's also steady and resilient. When I think of her, I think of *strength*. But as a girl, I think I sometimes misinterpreted this as a grin-and-bear-it attitude toward life—one where problems should be faced and solved without talking too much about them. Much of that was just me trying to figure things out, thinking that I could have the same approach to life as a teenager that she had gleaned from many years of experience.

Mom was ahead of her time in many ways. She loved yoga before it became something anyone could do at a number of local gyms. As a child, I used to watch her move into strange yoga positions while watching "The Late Show with David Letterman". I remember the first time I saw her in those funny positions. "Uh, Mom? Are you okay?" I didn't understand what yoga was about back then, but yoga would later become one of my greatest tools for healing—a pathway to inner-strength and resiliency that I would need so much of down the road.

My parents gave me so much. They showed me how to build a meaningful life, how to work hard, and how to live with purpose. They taught me how to be strong and gave me almost every tool I'd need to succeed in college and beyond. But something I didn't learn until many years later was how to be vulnerable. Some lessons in life are things you can only learn the hard way. Ultimately, vulnerability was exactly what I would need to face what would happen to me a few years later.

In all, my parents had three children. My older sister is my role model. She's always been someone I admired. I even used to think she was perfect. She had beautiful curly hair. She was always working out to stay in impeccable shape. She was confident, glamorous, and always polished—a stark contrast to me with my usual oversized Houston Rockets t-shirt (I was a big fan of Clyde Drexler and Hakeem Olajuwon) and comfy basketball shorts. In many ways, we were opposites, but we've always been close. She studied at Duke, and now she's a loving aunt to my kids, and the person I call when I just can't figure something out.

My brother is six years younger than me. In my mind, I've always been his caretaker. I carried him everywhere—so much so, in fact, that I remember my mom once telling me that he'd never learn to walk so long as I didn't let him even try! But learn to walk, he did. Today, he's a professional chef, food content editor, and social influencer. Just like Dad, he began down a path to law school. And just like Dad, he quit to pursue something he was even more passionate about.

Smashed between these two siblings, I was the family's free spirit. I wasn't afraid to stir things up. I was rebellious, independent, and always ready for a little trouble. I threw parties at my parents' house when they were out of town and sometimes made decisions I'd later regret. I wasn't a follower of trends or cliques. Instead, I found my people in those who embraced life with a sense of freedom, whether it was skateboarding, fishing, or listening to Texas country music.

You might have guessed that school wasn't my favorite place. I wasn't part of the "in" crowd. In fact, I often felt targeted by "mean girls." At the time, it hurt. Like most young girls, I took the drama very seriously. My teachers noticed this about me (and probably about other girls, too). I remember one elementary school teacher, Mrs. Hartman, who took me under her wing. She saw how much I was struggling with confidence, and sent me home one day with a cassette of Mariah Carey's "Hero." I remember locking myself in my room that night playing the song over and over and over again. I cried my heart out. It spoke to my soul. The idea that I could be my own hero was something I clung to then and still carry with me today.

Middle school introduced me to basketball, and I fell in love with the sport. I started to live, breathe, and love the sport. But when I didn't make the high school "A Team," my heart shattered. I made the "B Team," but I was so devastated that I didn't even want to play. My enterprising dad, ever the optimist, suggested we form our own team, and "the Lady Warriors" were born. That was one of the most diverse and enriching experiences of my childhood. I remember riding in a bus to Galveston to play in a tournament one weekend. Lots of my teammates had never seen the ocean! Everything we did together became a transformative experience. They taught me to appreciate the detours, and even find joy in life's unexpected turns. My dad made sure we knew to treat everyone on the team—as well as everyone around us—with dignity and respect. He taught me to open my eyes and see joy with this basketball team, instead of disappointment with myself. Through that team, I learned about joy in unexpected places, and my dad's wisdom—to always look for the good—became even more real to me.

In high school, friendships for me were always about quality, not quantity. I developed a tight-knit group of friends, and many of those relationships have lasted to this day. When I wasn't hanging out with them, I spent my time with the neighborhood boys. They weren't interested in gossip or cliques. They were more about adventure, and that suited me just fine.

I remember, as high school came to a close, I was feeling ready for something totally new. I'd gained some confidence, and I wanted to break free—to see the world beyond Texas. My parents took me to visit Arizona State University, and I felt from the moment I visited the campus that it was where I was meant to be. I graduated high school and began preparing for life away from home.

I can remember, as that last summer before college wound down, my mom played "Wide Open Spaces" by the Dixie Chicks on repeat. I never actually saw her

## Innocence

cry, but every time that song came on while we drove together, I noticed her eyes would mist, just barely. It was a quiet signal that she knew—it was time. My time. My parents had raised me in the most incredible way, and now it was my turn to spread my wings. So off to Arizona State I went, buzzing with excitement and possibility.

My mom helped me move into my dorm on a sweltering August Arizona day. The room was a tiny, two-room space shared with three other girls. It was a sweltering Arizona day, the kind of heat that presses down on you. The dorm buzzed with the energy of new beginnings. My roommate, whom I'd never met before, was the opposite of me. I was loud, outgoing, and ready for adventure. She was quiet, reserved, and preferred solitude. Sharing that small space with a stranger was a challenge, but I felt grateful to be there, on the edge of something new.

My mom, being the meticulous organizer she is (a trait I definitely didn't inherit), helped me make the most of the tiny closet. She set up my space so that I felt not just organized but secure, like I had a little slice of home with me. Before she left, she handed me a small ragdoll in a white baby-doll outfit—something my grandmother had given me before she passed. It was such a small thing, but when I held it, tears welled up. That little doll felt like a connection to my past and a reminder that no matter how far I traveled, I carried home with me.

When my mom gave me that final hug before she left, her face was calm as always, but I know in my heart she cried as she walked away.

I went back to my room and immediately felt a swirl of emotion. I was anxious and sad, but also excited. It was finally happening. I was starting my journey. Most of my friends had stayed in Texas, but not me. I was free, and I could feel it in my bones.

I loved every minute of my freshman year at ASU. But school work quickly became secondary to the thrill of new friends and the freedom of living on my own. I was happy, really happy, even if I wasn't the best at balancing fun and responsibility. I never saw myself as the type to join a sorority—chanting and the whole girlie-girl scene just wasn't me. But making friends in such a big school was harder than I expected, so I caved and rushed to a sorority. I wasn't super active in the sorority, but I'm still grateful for the friendships that came from it.

Oddly enough, I found a better fit with a fraternity. That's where I felt most at home. They even inducted me as "Brother Ashley," complete with a secret handshake and all. And no, I wasn't promiscuous with the guys. I was there to have fun and enjoy life. But underneath it all, I was insecure—just like so many freshmen. I felt a little lost, unsure of who I was or what I wanted to do with my life.

Looking back, I realize how deeply I was stuck in people-pleasing mode. I wanted so badly to fit in that I lost sight of myself and my own goals. It's a pattern that's followed me for much of my life. But things were working out in their own sort of way. I was still young, and I'd made some big strides as an independent girl out on her own. I knew my family back home loved me, and I had made friends who'd stick with me, even as insecure as I was on the inside.

But then, just as I was finding my rhythm, everything changed.

# 2

# Darkness

*"She walks the hills in a long black veil, ... nobody knows, nobody sees, nobody knows but me."*

IN A PARALLEL universe, a man named Kevin Lee Francois was living a life of darkness—a life filled with heinous acts of rape, and, according to his own family, likely murder.

His history of burglary, sexual assault, and voyeurism hadn't yet caught up to him. On the surface, he was a husband, a father, a son, and a brother—a man who seemed to be part of a family and a community. But Kevin was living a double life. By day, he worked as a painter in Orange and Los Angeles counties. He traveled often, but his private life was a much different story.

There was a storage shed on Kevin's property. Inside, it held a haunting collection—worn panties, and over three hundred school- and government-issued photo IDs, locked away in secret. At that point, the headlines hadn't been written. The people he had violated and traumatized hadn't come forward. No convictions had been handed down. Kevin hadn't served time for the damage he had caused. He continued to move through life untouched by the consequences of his actions.

We don't know what Kevin's early life looked like. We don't know the challenges he faced, the traumas he experienced, or the connections that shaped his twisted path. We don't know the moments that built up and fractured his mind, leading him down such a destructive road. His backstory is unclear. We know nothing of the shifts, the achievements, or the setbacks that may have contributed to the person he became. The pieces are missing, the picture incomplete.

What we do know comes from the stories of those who knew him—family members and high school classmates who would later drive hundreds of miles to "watch him fry." The bitterness and anger they carried were palpable.

In a 2010 statement issued by the California Department of Justice, it became clear that Kevin Lee Francois primarily preyed on college-age women, targeting those who lived near campuses. The police suspected that he had a pattern—breaking into homes and returning later to assault the residents. His movements weren't just limited to small neighborhoods either. Francois attended major sporting events all over the world—events like the Olympics, the Final Four College Basketball Tournament, and the Super Bowl. He blended into the crowd, seemingly living the life of a sports enthusiast, without anyone knowing the darkness lurking beneath.

On the surface, Kevin appeared to be living a "normal life." There was no outward sign of guilt, no visible fear that his past might catch up with him. He moved through the world, undeterred by the harm he had caused.

But fate, as it so often does, had other plans for Kevin Lee Francois.

# 3

# Intuition and Fate

INTUITION IS THE voice of our inner knowing. It's not something you can learn from a textbook or study—it's something you feel, something you sense deep inside. I've always had a strong intuition, though it's taken years of practice to truly listen to it. One evening, that intuition gave me a sharp, unmistakable warning. But this time, there was nothing I could do to stop what was coming. This time, it was my fate.

It was a warm August night in 2003. The sky was painted in breathtaking shades of pink, as though God himself had dipped a brush into the clouds at that very moment. I was about to start my sophomore year at Arizona State University, and I had arrived early to move into my new apartment, get settled, and get to know my new roommate. We had been placed in the very back corner of the complex, in Unit K on the ground floor. It was quiet, almost too quiet, isolated and overlooking an empty parking lot bordered by a fence, with only a neighborhood of trees beyond. Most students hadn't returned yet.

That night, I was looking forward to reuniting with my girlfriends. But before heading out, I did what I always did—I called my mom. She was my best friend, my anchor. I stood on the porch, watching the sun dip lower in the sky, giving her an update on everything. But as we were about to say goodbye, something shifted inside me. A deep, sharp feeling settled into my stomach—not the usual anxiety that sits high in your chest, but something deeper, heavier, a knowing that something was terribly wrong.

The feeling was so strong that I didn't want to hang up the phone. I hesitated, lingering in that moment, trying to understand what my intuition was telling me. But I told my mom I loved her, and I did what I always did—I hung up.

After I hung up the phone, the intensity of that feeling wouldn't leave me. It gnawed at me, a warning I couldn't quite place. I thought, maybe I'd get into some minor trouble that night, doing what nineteen-year-olds do. But I had no idea that the premonition I felt wasn't just a passing anxiety. It was the beginning of something that would shatter my life into a million tragic pieces.

## Intuition and Fate

The sky, once pink and beautiful, began to darken, but that uneasy feeling lingered, heavy in my body. As I left the house, it stayed with me, a shadow I couldn't shake.

I've always kept a small circle of girlfriends, but they're the best of the best. I've never been about quantity, only quality. To me, the best are rare, and I'm lucky enough to be surrounded by them. They're the kind of friends who avoid drama and are there when it counts. They're the ones who hold your hand and wipe your tears, the ones who'll drive around for hours, belting out your favorite songs with you. They're the friends who make you laugh until you cry, who hide your phone so you don't call your ex at 2 a.m., and who bring out the absolute best in you (and let's be real, maybe a little bit of the wild side too).

These are the friends you still have slumber parties with well into your thirties and forties. The ones you dream of living with in a Golden Girls-style commune when you're old. They're the ones who would drop everything in a heartbeat if you needed them, the ones who show up for you in your darkest hour. These are my girls. And if you have friends like this, you know how lucky I feel to have them in my life.

These women hold my heart forever. We met our freshman year at Arizona State, and I honestly don't think I would have survived what I went through without them. As I write this, tears fill my eyes because they are a part of what I now call "Ashley's Angels"—the people whose love and support have carried me through the hardest moments of my life.

At the start of our sophomore year, we were all so young and carefree, excited to be reunited after the summer. That first week, I was eager to meet my new roommate and settle into our apartment. The campus energy hadn't picked up yet; the air was still quiet and unhurried. The apartment complex was huge, with a wide open gate and towering trees that stretched toward the sky. My apartment, tucked into the far back corner, was in Building K, on the ground floor. My roommate took the master bedroom, and I had the smaller room near the front door, with windows facing the street and a small bathroom off to the side.

The campus still felt desolate, like it was holding its breath before the rush of students filled the space. We'd only been there a week, and my roommate already seemed to have frequent male visitors stopping by. It wasn't long before the layout of our apartment was familiar to more people than I was comfortable with.

## Intuition and Fate

That first week, after I had settled in, my girlfriends and I went out to celebrate one of our friends' birthdays. We were bursting with excitement about the year ahead—we'd missed each other so much over the summer. By the time we got back to my apartment, it was late. My roommate and her new boyfriend were still awake, but they eventually went off to her room to sleep.

The girls and I stayed up talking, as we always did. One of my friends had suffered a terrible loss in high school, so we spent the night comforting her, listening and being there for her in the way only close friends can. Time slipped away from us, and it was well past midnight when we realized how late it was. I told them they should just stay the night—there was no rush to leave—but one by one, they decided to head home.

After everyone left, I called my mom, like I always did. "Mom, I have a rush meeting tomorrow morning. Please call me, okay? I need you to be my alarm—I can't oversleep!" My mom had been my alarm clock for as long as I could remember, even into college. Bless her heart, she probably thought those days were behind her. But she agreed, even though I could tell she was tired. "Go to bed," she said softly. "I love you, Mom," I told her as I hung up the phone.

I put my Norah Jones CD into the player and let her voice carry me to sleep. I felt happy and safe in my new home... or at least, I thought I was. Looking back, I remember how my intuition had tried to tell me something was off, but the events that followed were already in motion. They were out of my hands. It was my fate.

# 4

# Tragedy

WARNING: THIS CHAPTER is difficult to write, and I know it will be difficult to read. In this chapter, I describe the brutal assault I endured when I was nineteen. I want to be upfront—the journey I'm about to take you on is dark. It's a journey of survival, but also one of deep pain, one where I lost my way and couldn't find the light for a long time. I will share with you the intense, debilitating anxiety, the paralyzing fear, the depression, shame, and self-hate that followed in the aftermath.

I will speak of the man who did this to me—a serial rapist. His arrest in Newport Beach, just blocks from my home, would eventually bring some closure, but the impact of that night reverberated through my life in ways I couldn't have imagined. I will also talk about the lasting effects—how it shattered my relationship with my body, how I came to hate sex, and how it led me down a path into an abusive, unhealthy relationship. I felt broken. Ashamed. Angry as hell. Somewhere along the way, I lost sight of the divine beauty within me. I lost sight of the light.

This chapter is about that darkness, but it's also about what I can see now that I couldn't see then. If these topics are triggering for you, please take care of yourself. I truly believe our triggers are also our teachers, but that doesn't mean you have to push through all at once. Know that I'm writing this with love, hoping to connect with your story, too. If it gets too heavy, take breaks. As one of my teachers always says, "Feel your feet on the ground. Open your eyes. Look around. Listen to the sounds. See how far you've come. You survived. You are safe."

And remember, in order to heal, we have to be brave enough to face the darkness. My favorite song by Florence and the Machine has a line that I hold close: "It's always darkest before the dawn." After all the darkness, light always follows.

～

August 22, 2003, was one of those sweltering Arizona summer nights, the kind where the heat lingers long after the sun has dipped below the horizon. I was sitting out on the patio of our apartment, tucked into the back corner of the lot, talking to my mom on the phone. The sky was

## Tragedy

painted in breathtaking shades of red, orange, and pink before fading into purples and deep blues. The sun was setting quickly, and darkness was creeping in.

In those days, my mom had become more than just my mother—she had become my best friend. College had brought us closer than ever before. It was a normal conversation, nothing remarkable or particularly memorable. But even as we talked, something deep inside me felt off. It wasn't anxiety; I knew that feeling too well—light, dizzy, racing heart, racing thoughts. This was different. There was a heaviness in my gut, a sinking feeling I couldn't shake. My intuition was screaming that something was terribly wrong.

When it was time to say goodbye, I didn't want to hang up the phone. Something inside me didn't want to let go. But eventually, we said our goodnights. And just like that, the sky was completely dark.

That was the night I described in the previous chapter. I went out with my best girlfriends, and after a fun night, we all came back to my apartment in a cab. We stayed up late, talking the way only close friends can. I invited them to stay over a couple of times, but one by one, they decided to head home. It was during sorority rush, and we all had early mornings ahead.

As I shared before, I put on my Norah Jones CD, called my mom and asked her to be my alarm clock for the morning—something she had done for me all my life. I drifted off to sleep with the babydoll my grandmother had given me, feeling comforted by her memory.

I've always slept on my stomach, with a pillow behind my head to block out any noise or light. It's just how I've always slept, never thinking much of it. That night was no different. I went to bed in the same way I had done countless times before. But what I didn't know was that, in mere moments, my entire life was about to be shattered.

An intruder had made his way into my apartment—into my bed. I remember the moment I felt him there, ripping my clothes off from the waist down. He pressed a pillow over my face, smothering me, suffocating me. For a brief moment, I thought I must be dreaming. It had to be a nightmare, right? But then the terror crept in—the horror that this wasn't a dream. This was happening. I kept telling myself, Wake up! Wake up! But I couldn't breathe. I couldn't move. My mind raced, but my body was trapped. It was then that I realized I was going to have to fight for my life.

He held the pillow over my face, cutting off my air, beating me while I struggled underneath him. I frantically moved my chin, trying to find some breath, but there was no air. I can't breathe! My mind screamed it, but no sound came out. I was suffocating. And then it hit me—I had two choices: to keep fighting and die, or to let it happen and maybe, just maybe, live. All I wanted in that moment was to survive.

For hours, I was violently raped—tortured in ways I didn't even know were possible. There are no words to describe the depths of that pain. As he assaulted me, he taunted me, talking about the other girls he had been watching. He knew what we had been wearing. He threatened to silence me. He said he would kill me if I ever told anyone. All of this happened in total darkness, the pillow pressed against my face. I couldn't see. I couldn't move. And I didn't think I was going to survive.

My bed was right next to the window, the headboard pressed against the wall. At some point, through the blur of terror, I felt him pause. I could barely lift my head, but I saw two fingers peel back the plastic blinds. In that moment, I realized it was morning. The sun had risen. How could no one have heard me? Where was everyone?

He opened and closed the blinds. Then, I felt him crawl off my body. I began to shake uncontrollably, my whole body trembling. But for the first time all night,

I felt a flicker of hope—like I might actually live, like I might make it through.

I heard him getting dressed, and dared not move.

"DO NOT REMOVE THE PILLOW FROM YOUR FACE," he said.

"DO NOT TELL ANYONE."

"I WILL BE WATCHING YOU."

"IF YOU DO TELL ANYONE I WILL KILL YOU."

I was as silent as I could be.

I thought if I didn't move, I might live.

Using my intuition, I sensed when he left my apartment, then frantically threw the covers off, slammed my bedroom door shut, locked it, and frantically put clothes on.

I looked for my cell phone.

It was nowhere to be found.

I wanted to get the hell out of my bedroom.

I broke the window, jumped out of my room, ran around to the side, jumped over the patio wall that was outside the master bedroom where my roommate was still sleeping with her boyfriend.

I started screaming, "I've been raped, call 911!" over and over.

My roommate opened the patio door.

# Tragedy

Blood was dripping down my entire body.

They were both as white as a ghost.

They had no idea what they were looking at.

They were experiencing deep shock too.

My roommate called 911.

I waited outside.

I didn't ever want to feel trapped again.

I paced the parking lot.

There were no cars around, no one was driving by.

It was still early, still desolate and empty.

The sun was rising.

After I screamed for them to call 911, the first thing I said was that I wanted to call my mom.

It felt like years waiting for law enforcement to arrive. I have no concept of the actual time but it felt painfully, horrifically slow. Standing in the corner in the back of the parking lot by my apartment, I finally saw a police car drive up. When he pulled up next to me, we locked eyes and he saw the state I was in. He mouthed the words, "Oh my god."

Everything became a blur. I was numb.

The police officer was kind and gentle. His name was Officer Williams. He made me feel believed, and calmed me.

He saved my life.

He knew we had to act fast.

I was sitting at the front of the apartment when a fire truck pulled up. As it approached, I realized something strange—I wasn't fully in my body. My consciousness had drifted, and I found myself watching everything from above, detached, as though I were hovering over the scene. From this distance, I saw the fireman pointing to my face, asking, "Is this where you were hit?" I watched as my head nodded in response, but it didn't feel like me. There were no words, no voice—I couldn't speak. All I could do was nod.

Most of that time is a blur. My memory comes and goes in fragments, as if I was floating in and out of awareness. One moment, I was sitting there. Next, I was inside the apartment with a police officer. I looked around, still trying to piece it all together, and the first thing I noticed was the barricade in front of my roommate's door—a barstool and a few pillows wedged tightly under the handle, holding it shut.

In that instant, the reality hit me hard. If she had tried to get out while he was attacking me, she would've made noise. The barstool scraping against the floor, the door struggling against the pillows—it would've alerted him.

## Tragedy

He would've heard, and he would've had time to escape. The thought sent a wave of realization through me—how close everything was, how fragile that moment had been.

Officer Williams calmly explained that we needed to get to the clinic, that evidence had to be collected from my body for a rape kit. At that point in my life, I had no idea what he was talking about. I hadn't heard the language he was using—I didn't know what a rape kit was. I hadn't seen shows like CSI, and forensic DNA wasn't something I'd ever even considered. I had no clue what you were supposed to do if you were raped. It just wasn't something that was ever discussed at home or school.

When he told me I needed to go to the clinic, my immediate reaction was to raise my voice in disgust. "Before I go anywhere, I need to shower. I need to change my clothes." I couldn't bear the feeling of my skin, the weight of the tank top clinging to my body. I wanted to brush my teeth. I felt absolutely filthy—wretched, actually. But they gently told me that I couldn't shower, couldn't change, couldn't brush my teeth. The very things I thought would make me feel human again were out of reach. Still, they reassured me, promising I would be safe as they took me to have the examination done.

If it hadn't been for Officer Williams, I don't think I would have stepped foot in that van. But he treated me with such empathy, with such deep compassion, that I felt like I could trust him. In that moment of intense trauma, he made me feel believed. He seemed seven feet tall, like a guardian angel, standing there with his calm presence and care. It was because of him that I found the courage to take the next step, to have the sexual assault nurse examination.

My wish, my hope, is that one day every survivor will be met with an Officer Williams—a protector who sees them, believes them, and helps them take that brave next step. We hear so much negativity in the news about law enforcement, and I get it, but what we don't hear about are the heroes like Officer Williams, the ones who risk their lives to protect us, to make our communities safer. He is one of my heroes.

On the way to the clinic, my body gave in to that familiar out-of-body sensation. Once again, I floated up and away, watching from above as we arrived at the clinic, disconnected from the world below.

I had just endured a violent sexual assault and a brutal home invasion, and now I was being asked to step into a cold, sterile room. The gown they gave me, with its open back, left me feeling completely exposed and vulnerable. I had to undress entirely, and my body—already feeling violated—was about to be examined again. This time, though, it wasn't for survival. This time, it was for evidence. They needed to swab and photograph my entire body, inside and out. Every bruise, every tear, every exposed piece of tissue, every caked inch of dried blood. It felt dark and invasive, like I was being violated all over again. I can understand now why many survivors would want to avoid this exam in the aftermath of such horror.

The forensic nurse assigned to my case was named Jennifer. She had dark brown hair, and there was something calming about her presence. She was gentle, but she was also strong. I was terrified. Humiliated. Broken. I felt disgusted with my body and completely detached from it, like I wasn't even there—just floating above, watching it all happen to someone else. But my dad had always taught me to look for the light, and in that dark, sterile room, my soul recognized something in Jennifer. She was providing a safe space, and even in my brokenness, I could feel it.

I still remember vividly how Jennifer made me feel. She didn't rush. She didn't take over. Instead, she asked my permission before every single step, making sure I felt safe and as calm as I could be. In a situation where I had no control, she gave me a small piece of it back. In retrospect, I realize that what Jennifer did for me wasn't just about collecting evidence—it was one of my first baby steps toward healing.

At the time, I didn't have the language for it, but Jennifer's care was a gift. She was a true angel in that moment, and she gave me a sense of healing when I didn't even know what healing was. For a brief moment in time, in her presence, my soul felt a flicker of peace.

I need to acknowledge something important—there are many victims out there who won't know what to do, won't know what to ask, and won't know where to go after an assault. Many will end up in hospitals where the staff isn't trained in trauma-informed care, where the collection of evidence isn't handled with the respect and kindness it requires. Some victims won't move forward with law enforcement at all, and that's their choice. And in too many rural towns, there aren't staff members who understand the psychological care that needs to accompany evidence collection, the way Jennifer did for me.

It is always the victim's choice whether or not to move forward with collecting evidence. For those who do, know that many clinics offer more than just evidence collection. They can provide access to medications for sexually transmitted infections, the morning-after pill, and the emotional support that comes from working with professionals who are trained in this area of trauma. And while collecting evidence is often thought of as something tied to pressing charges, it doesn't have to be. It can be part of your own personal healing journey—an opportunity to reclaim some sense of control.

When my exam was over, I got dressed, though I'll be honest, much of this time is a blur. My memory is hazy, not because I was under any influence, but because trauma has a way of creating a kind of delirium that can last for a long time. But there is one moment I remember vividly: Jennifer placed her hand gently on my shoulder as I was about to leave the exam room. She looked at me with so much compassion and said, "Ashley, this is horrible, what has happened to you. But don't let what this man did define you or your life." Tears filled my eyes, and I nodded, even though at the time, I wasn't sure how not to let it define me.

As I walked out the door, I was met by both of my parents. They were there, standing together, and immediately took me under their wings. I remember thinking,

How did they get here so fast? Did they teleport? Was this some kind of *Back to the Future* moment? But what I knew for certain was how grateful I was. In that moment, I realized how fortunate I was to have their love and support.

My roommate was there with my parents. We all piled into the same car, heading to a hotel my parents had booked for us. We had to pull over several times because my roommate kept getting sick. Looking back, I realize now with deep empathy that rape doesn't just impact the person it happens to—it ripples out, breaking down the people around them, affecting the entire community. Trauma doesn't exist in isolation.

That night, it was just me and my parents in the hotel. Their suite was connected to mine. My mom gave me the sedatives, the morning-after pill, and the other medications from the clinic. Somehow, I managed to fall asleep. But it wasn't peaceful, and it didn't last long. Almost immediately, I began to relive the nightmare of my assault in my dreams. But this time, something was different—I was able to shake myself awake. I woke up drenched in sweat, tears streaming down my face.

And yet, this time, when I woke from the nightmare, I wasn't alone. I was surrounded by love. All the girls who

## Tragedy

had been at my apartment earlier that night were now with me, squeezed into the king-sized hotel bed. I hadn't even known they were aware of what had happened to me, let alone that it was already all over the local news. But while I slept, my parents had reached out to them, and they came, showing up to support me in the way only true friends can. Their presence, their love—it was healing in a way I hadn't known I needed.

At first, I sprinted out of the bed, thinking I was still in danger, that it was all happening again. But they were there to pull me out of it, to remind me I was safe, that I was okay.

Looking back now, I can see how much it took to get me through that night. The police, forensic nurse Jennifer, my friends, my parents—they all played a part in giving me the strength to survive.

Growing up in Austin, Ann Richards was a prominent figure in Texas politics and a dear friend of my dad's. He always loved to tell the story of how, whenever things weren't going well, Ann would kiss him on the cheek and say, "Precious, get over it and get on with it." It's a sentiment that stayed with me—simple, direct, and, in its own way, filled with love. Though my journey was far from over, I carried that strength with me, from those who showed up when I needed it most.

So, a few days later at the hotel, I decided to take the first step in reclaiming some part of myself. I told myself I was going to work out. Alone. Just the thought of walking by myself to the gym was terrifying for all of us—my friends, my family, and especially me. Fear, trauma, and rage were bubbling up in my soul, but I knew I needed this. I needed to be by myself. My friends wanted to come with me, to keep me safe, but I was clear that I had to do this on my own. I had to take back a little piece of independence, a sliver of strength.

I put on my headphones—the old-school kind that went over your head and plugged into a CD player—and blasted Christina Aguilera's "Fighter" on repeat. That song lit something inside me. In my brokenness, in my fear, rage became my power. Christina became one of my heroes in those moments. Her voice, that song—it helped save my life. It gave me strength when I had none.

I'd crank up the volume, hop on the elliptical, and with each step, I pressed down with the force of hell's fury. There were moments when I pushed so hard that the pedals actually flew off their tracks. I was angry—angrier than I'd ever been—but in that anger, I found some kind of release.

After my workouts, I'd return to the hotel room and switch to another song—"Oooh Child (Things Are Gonna Get Easier)". I didn't know if things would actually get easier, but I clung to that hope. Then, I'd cry. I cried so hard I didn't think I had any more tears to shed. Every time I thought I had hit the bottom, more would come. The tears felt endless, like there was no end to the grief, no end to the pain. As the days went on, it only seemed to get worse.

I couldn't see any light during that time. The anger helped me survive, and the music gave me an outlet, but I was in a very dark place. My friends were there, my parents were there, and they helped me hold on. But the darkness was overwhelming.

I didn't know if we'd ever catch him.

I wondered if I would live in fear and anger for the rest of my life.

I didn't know if the nightmares would ever stop, if I would ever sleep peacefully again.

I didn't think I'd ever feel safe in my body.

Worst of all, I didn't know if the perpetrator would follow through on his promise to kill me.

# 5

# Fighter

*You tried to hide your lies, disguise yourself*
*Through living in Denial*
*But in the end you'll see, you won't stop me*
*I am a fighter*
*I ain't gonna stop*
*There is no turning back*
—Christina Aguilera

JUST A FEW days after the assault, I went back to school at Arizona State University, trying to reclaim some sense of normalcy. But as soon as I sat down in class, with bruises still visible all over my face, neck, and body, I was debilitated by a panic attack. My chest tightened so much that I could barely breathe. I had to run outside, gasping for air. *Is he watching me?* I thought. *Is he sitting behind me? Following me at the grocery store? Waiting to do it again?* The fear was suffocating. *The assault had been all over the news—has he seen it? Is he going to kill me?*

I knew this man had been watching me. He had told me during the attack that he knew what I was wearing, what my friends were wearing. That knowledge haunted me. I couldn't even wash my face because it meant closing my eyes, and I couldn't bear the thought of not knowing who might be standing behind me at that moment. The fear of being caught off guard again was paralyzing—and it infuriated me.

But just like Christina Aguilera's lyrics, I became a fighter. Every day, I went to battle—fighting for justice, fighting to catch the man who did this to me.

I worked tirelessly with detectives. I would call and confront suspects over the phone, accusing them, retracing every step of the night, trying to convince them to give DNA samples. Some refused, so the detectives would meet them at local bars, gathering DNA from discarded glasses, looking for any lead that would crack the case. But time and again, the leads went nowhere. The fight drained me, and with every dead end, my heart broke a little more.

Eventually, the fighter in me couldn't do it anymore. I couldn't focus. I couldn't sleep. The hope of ever catching the monster who had broken into my home and brutally assaulted me was slipping away. I had worn my fierce strength like armor, numbing myself to the pain underneath. But inside, I was slowly dying. The anger, the fight, the unrelenting pursuit of justice—it was all hiding the deeper truth. I was hurting, deeply. I was losing myself in the battle.

I talked to someone at the school about what had happened, and the response was... strange. There was a lack of empathy that I hadn't expected. Maybe they were worried the school might be held accountable, even though I was living off campus. But what I remember most was how alone I felt in that conversation. I told them I had to drop out. I couldn't keep going—not mentally, not emotionally. I was exhausted from sleepless nights, from living in constant fear.

I just couldn't do it anymore.

I had really liked ASU, and I had tried so hard to make it work, but I was a victim there. My story had been plastered all over the news. People knew about me, but they didn't know me. I just wanted to be me—Ashley. That ability to simply be myself in college, to be a student without the weight of this assault hanging over me, was taken from me the moment the attack happened.

And the worst part? There was no closure. The case was still open, the fear still present, and it left a bitter taste in my mouth about staying in Arizona. I knew in my heart that I couldn't stay. The fresh start I needed wasn't going to be found there.

My friend Gianna had been with me through it all—our whole freshman year and the attack. She was from Minnesota and had always dreamed of living by the beach. Her sister was already in Newport, and that's all we needed to know. Over winter break, we packed up Gianna's car, picked up, and moved to Newport Beach, California. We didn't tell anyone, didn't ask for permission. Our friends came back from winter break, and we were just gone.

I remember watching the "Welcome to Arizona" sign shrink in the rearview mirror, windows down, and the wind rushing through. We had no clear direction, but we weren't looking for one. We just wanted to feel free. More than anything, I wanted to close the chapter of my life that Arizona represented. In Newport Beach, I would just be Ashley. No one would know what had happened. I wouldn't be the victim anymore—I would just be me.

Gianna was behind the wheel, and she had her own pain. Her boyfriend had tragically passed away in high school, and she was still grieving, still lost. We bonded over our shared desire for inner happiness, a happiness we both knew we weren't going to find in Arizona. Our birthdays are just one day apart, and as two Pisces souls, we knew we belonged by the ocean. Gianna turned up the volume on "Goodbye Earl" by the Dixie Chicks, and with the windows down, the wind in our hair, we drove those six hours to the coast of Southern California.

We couldn't stop smiling—not just on our faces but from deep within our souls. It was a feeling of joy, the kind neither of us had felt in a long, long time. We had no idea where we were going, but we had each other. And that was enough. It felt like a scene from *Thelma and Louise*—the laughter, the uncertainty, the open road ahead of us.

But more than anything, we had hope. Hope for a better life, hope for a future that wasn't defined by our pasts. We weren't just escaping what was—we were creating something new. Not fate, but our own destiny.

When we first got to Newport, we stayed with Gianna's sister and her husband. They were so loving and gracious, letting us crash on their couch for what felt like forever. But eventually, as anyone would, they gently let us know it was time to find somewhere else. So, we moved to the Best Western.

We were living off our parents' support, but that didn't last long. When they cut us off from staying at the hotel, we had to figure something out. That's when we both started nannying for quadruplets. It wasn't easy, but it gave us a sense of purpose. Between nannying and going to community college, we were doing our best to get back on our feet.

We eventually found our own little beach house rental on 40th Street. Newport Beach truly is one of the cutest beach towns. People rode their beach cruisers everywhere, surfers dotted the coastline during the day, and by night, they traded their wetsuits for something a little dressier. We joined in, wearing high heels and riding our bikes along the boardwalk, feeling like we were slowly beginning to heal. The ocean had that effect on us. Being by the water felt so good—natural, even. It was healing, just like we always knew it would be. As two Pisces, the water was our refuge.

But while I was reinventing myself in this new life, I made a firm decision: no one here would know what happened to me in Arizona. I wouldn't talk about it. I was determined to just be me—not the victim, not the girl with the past. I thought this was strength, but in reality, I was burying my pain. I didn't realize how much I was hurting by not talking about it. That suppression took me down a dangerous path.

I started to numb everything out. I used alcohol to dull the fear, and I got a Xanax prescription by making up a story about being afraid to fly. The numbing became my shield. I even began taking NyQuil during the day, just trying to catch some sleep, desperate for some kind of relief from the exhaustion of pretending I was fine. But I wasn't. I had no closure. The fear was still there, lurking behind every moment of silence, even though I was pretending it wasn't.

On the outside, I looked like I was rebuilding—working, going to school, smiling, trying to live a new life. But inside, I was falling apart. I couldn't shake the thought that as long as the perpetrator was still out there, I wasn't his last victim. Someone else was going to suffer, someone else was going to be tortured, raped, maybe even killed. That weight stayed with me, pressing down, while I tried to keep my head above water.

My life began to spiral out of control again. I was lost—completely disconnected from myself and from any sense of stability. God bless my roommate and her boyfriend, who stood by me through one of the darkest times of my life. To this day, I carry a sense of remorse for the pain and chaos I unintentionally inflicted on them, and on all the people who loved me during that time. I didn't know how to cope. My soul was lost, and I couldn't see a way out.

There were two different occasions when I woke up on the couch downstairs, a hospital band around my wrist with my name on it. My body ached, and everything was hazy, like I was swimming through thick fog. I couldn't remember how I got there. I had no memory of the emergency workers who picked me up from a bar, took me to the hospital, and then sent me home. I had no idea what had happened. It felt like everything—drugs, depression, and some kind of darkness—was closing in on me. I was suffocating.

It was terrifying, and I knew deep down that something had to change. I couldn't keep living like this. I couldn't keep hurting myself and the people around me. There was no way forward if I continued on this path. Something had to shift, and I knew it had to start with me.

# 6

# Surrender

EARLIER, I MENTIONED that my mom was a yogi. Every night, she'd practice yoga while watching "The Late Show with David Letterman". I never quite understood it—why she was breathing so deeply, puffing her belly out and then snapping it back so quickly. It was strange to me, and to be honest, it always freaked me out a little to watch her do yoga and meditate. But looking back, it was a glimpse of what would eventually become a major part of my own healing journey.

At this point in my life, my roommate was running low on patience. I was a lot to handle, and I know I wasn't easy to be around. One day, she suggested I try going to YogaWorks in Costa Mesa. It was just a couple of miles inland from Newport Beach, and it was a well-known chain of yoga studios in the area. She didn't just suggest it—she begged, then practically dragged me there. Maybe I agreed more for her sake than for my own sanity, but I finally decided to give it a try.

She drove us off the peninsula, and as we headed into Costa Mesa, I remember the beautiful palm trees lining the streets, the bright California sunshine streaming through the car window. Everything around me looked peaceful, calm, and radiant. And yet, inside, I was anxious. I had been living in a near-constant state of debilitating anxiety since my attack, and this—going to a yoga class—added another layer of discomfort.

We pulled into the parking lot of a strip mall, and I saw the YogaWorks sign up on the second story, just past the outdoor stairs. My heart raced, my mind spiraled. But I got out of the car, took a deep breath, and made my way toward the entrance. I didn't know it at the time, but this was the beginning of a chapter in my healing I hadn't yet imagined.

Walking into the studio, the smell of incense hit us immediately. It was overpowering, and everything about the space felt awkward. I was still so detached from my body, so disgusted with it. Ever since the rape, I had carried a deep sense of shame and discomfort in my own skin. The thought of doing anything that would bring me closer to my body was repulsive. I hated it—this body that no longer felt like mine. It felt damaged, foreign, used. It felt disgusting.

I grabbed a rental mat from the front desk and made my way to the far back corner of the room. The class was crowded, and I didn't want to be seen. I didn't want anyone to notice me. The windows were open, letting in a warm breeze, and there were no mirrors—no one could get behind me. I did everything I could to create some sense of safety for myself, but even then, it didn't feel good. I felt my heart start to race.

I was so uncomfortable, and I wanted to leave. I thought about walking out several times as I waited for class to begin. Then the door opened, and in walked Toni, our yoga teacher, and it was like an angel had entered the room. She had big, beautiful curly hair, a vibrant tan, and a smile so bright it lit up the entire space. You know those people who walk into a room and seem to light it up from the inside out? That was Toni.

At the start of class, Toni shared a story about her husband's battle with cancer. Her voice was calm and steady as she reminded us that we were all in different spaces, coming from different walks of life. She taught us to be present in our own practice, no matter where we were at that moment. I took a deep breath and decided to stay.

But it felt disastrous. I felt disconnected. Discombobulated. Completely out of place.

It was incredibly hard just to stay on my mat, to stay present in my body. But I made it through the class. And somehow, despite how uncomfortable it was, I kept going back—even without my roommate. I went alone to Toni's classes.

There was something about the warrior poses that began to heal me. In those postures, your feet are rooted firmly to the ground with power, your chest is lifted, and suddenly you feel this mix of courage, grace, and strength pulsing through you. As I spread my fingertips wide, I could feel the energy moving through my body—it was magnetic, powerful even. In yoga, they call this energy "stirah" and "sukha," which translates to strength and ease. It's a balance you find in your body, in your gaze, in the way you hold both power and softness at the same time. It's a dance that always reminds me of a goddess warrior—strong, yet sensual. Courageous and kind. And, yes, strong as hell.

For the first time since my attack, I began to feel a side of myself that I thought had been taken away. I remember thinking: maybe there is light. Maybe I am strong.

Airplane pose became another source of healing for me. In this pose, you press firmly into one foot, lifting the opposite leg behind you while your chest hinges forward, parallel to the earth. All four corners of your base foot are rooted into the mat. Your gaze, your drishti, is steady. You find balance in the pose, even when everything else feels shaky. At a time when my life felt so unclear—when I was numb and medicated—this pose gave me a sense of confidence and clarity. I felt sober. I felt alive. I felt like I was living again.

Then there's savasana—the final resting pose, where the healing really takes place. Yoga stirs up so much emotion, like shaking a snow globe. Savasana is the moment when everything settles, when stillness takes over. You lie flat on the floor, close your eyes, and let go. I like to think of it as "adult nap time." In savasana, something shifts. You let go of your breath, your thoughts—everything softens. It's the time when all the energy you've built up during practice begins to settle. And if you surrender deep enough, you can feel transported to another dimension, a place of peace and calm.

Toward the end of my eighth class with Toni, she guided us into savasana, the final resting pose. Up until that class, I had never truly been able to let go. Even though I positioned myself in the back corner of the room, I was always looking over my shoulder, always too tense to close my eyes and feel safe. Every fiber of my being was on high alert when I knew I should be resting.

As we laid down, the soft melody of the Beatles' "Let It Be" filled the room. The lyrics about Mother Mary hit me in just the right way—my own mom's name is Mary. It was like a wave of comfort washed over me, something that I hadn't felt in a long time. And for the first time, tears began to flow from the corners of my eyes onto the yoga mat beneath me. These weren't the same tears of despair and pain that I had been carrying since my rape. These were different. These were healing tears.

In that moment, there was a deep sense of knowing. I couldn't change what had happened to me, but I realized it wouldn't define me forever. A wave of peace came over me, a sense of surrender. I let go, and for the first time since my attack, I took a deep breath. I closed my eyes. I rested.

It occurred to me then that I had never even introduced myself to Toni. Yet here I was, finding peace and safety in this space that had once felt so foreign to me. I was resting—without alcohol, without Xanax, without any numbing agents—among complete strangers. And somehow, I felt safe.

My mom, Gianna, and yoga saved my life.

Yoga isn't for everyone. But it was for me. It is for me. Yoga became the tool that unlocked deep healing within me. But what I've come to realize is that there's something for everyone—something that will speak to each person in their own journey. In the coming chapter on healing, I'll share more of the gifts and tools that helped me, along with the beautiful synchronicities that have continued to guide me on this path.

# 7

# I Got the Call

IN 2007, I graduated from Chapman University. That same year, I met my husband and the father of my children in Newport Beach, California. He was kind, outgoing, and we always had a great time together. At that point in my life, I still didn't know who I was. I was detached—from my body, from my soul. But he made me feel safe, secure, like I was finally starting to turn my life around.

We wanted to move closer to my parents in Austin, to give back to them for everything they had given me.

Let me pause here to acknowledge something that's often overlooked: rape doesn't just affect the victim—it ripples through the whole family system and the entire community. My parents walked through that grief with me, every step of the way. So moving back to be near them felt like the right choice for the next season of my life.

In 2008, I moved back to Texas with Jason and our precious English bulldog, Grace. Grace was a bundle of love, with her white and brown fur, her smushed nose, and a tiny, stubby tail. She was so excited every time she saw us that her whole backside would wiggle—her tail was too small to do the job on its own. Grace became my protector in a way that felt almost spiritual. She always slept right beside me on the floor in her pink, plush dog bed, and the moment she heard a noise in the night, she'd spring up and race to the window, barking ferociously. Grace always had my back.

Once we settled in Austin, we were welcomed with open arms by my sister's friend group. We started having Sunday night dinners at my parents' house, a mix of Lebanese feasts and my dad's famous BBQ—especially his "Roy's ribs." Life felt full, like we were surrounded by love and community.

Jason and I eventually got married in Austin at the beautiful St. Mary's Cathedral. We were both raised Catholic, and it felt right. The wedding was followed by the most spectacular outdoor celebration in my parents' backyard, overlooking Lady Bird Lake and the Austin skyline. After so much darkness, we were finally celebrating joy.

But even in the midst of all that joy, there was still a heaviness deep inside. I chose never to speak of my attack, to live like it had never happened. On the outside, everything was perfect. But despite all the beautiful moments, there was a darkness that remained untapped in my soul, a part of me still carrying the weight of what I hadn't yet healed.

I kept doing yoga, battling my demons one breath, one pose at a time. But I didn't have the self-confidence to pursue yoga teacher training. I talked myself out of it, convinced I wasn't ready. After the attack, I had lost so much of my vibrant, outgoing nature. I became more reserved, more shy, more insecure. The parts of me that used to light up a room now felt dimmed.

But I still loved yoga. It was my refuge. I practiced three to four times a week while working at my father's advertising agency, GSD&M. The agency was known for its vibrant culture, its purpose-driven mission, and its fun, energetic environment. But there was no special treatment for me just because I was the boss's daughter. In fact, I remember being one of the only employees who had to work through Christmas break because I hadn't racked up enough vacation days. And honestly, I was grateful for that. I was treated like everyone else, and I appreciated the work. But still, I felt lost.

Before moving back to Texas, I had the chance to work for an online travel production company as an intern in California. The show was called "Around the World For Free," and it took me to places I had never imagined—like Vietnam. I remember being in Vietnam and feeling a spark ignite in my soul, a spark I hadn't felt in so long. I wanted more. I wanted to travel, but not the kind of travel where you stay in resorts and sip cocktails by the pool. I wanted to meet the people, live in their culture, dance with them, eat with them, experience the world as they did.

I knew I had so much to give, but deep down, I also knew my gifts weren't in marketing or advertising. My soul had its own calling, but I didn't know what that was yet. So, I stuck with it. I stayed the course, even though I felt that pull toward something more. I just didn't know what that "more" looked like.

But eventually, I came to understand that there was a divine purpose for my soul in this world—I just had to keep searching for it.

A few years after moving back to Austin, I was in the backyard with my husband and our dog, Grace, when the shocking news came in. My parents showed up at my house unexpectedly, and my dad had brought over some of his homemade Royito's Hot Sauce—one of the best hot sauces out there. I'd spent so many holidays at their lake house making hot sauce with my family, hours spent bottling it up to give as gifts to what felt like the entire city.

When my parents knocked on the door that day, I remember thinking it was strange that they just popped by unannounced. My dad stood there, grinning with his big smile, his small-town Texas accent coming through as he said, "Elizabeth"—my middle name, which he used mostly when I was in trouble or when he was feeling intense emotion—"I made you some fresh hot sauce."

I let them in, and we went out to the backyard. Grace was there, chewing on those small white flowers she loved. She was always by my side, in some way or another.

Then, out of nowhere, my mom gently touched my arm, and what felt like lightning struck me. Her words hit like a shockwave. "We got a call today from the detectives. There was a DNA match in your case. He's been arrested."

My body froze.

To give a little background, after all these years, while I had somewhat given up hope, my parents and the incredible detectives working my case never did. When they made the arrest, the first person the detective called was my mom.

I stood there, in total shock and disbelief, feeling the color drain from my face. I never thought this day would come, and now it had. There was a DNA match in my case. After seven long years of not knowing who had done this to me—seven years of knowing he was still out there, hurting others—it felt surreal.

A wave of relief hit me first. Maybe, just maybe, he would never hurt another person again.

But right behind that relief came fury. My relief quickly turned into boiling hot anger. I could feel the blood rising to the surface of my skin, like a fire had been lit inside me. *Why now?* I thought. After all these years, after pulling myself out of the gates of hell, after fighting so hard for healing, after working tirelessly to move on with my life—why now? Now it was all coming back. All the pain, the memories, the trauma. It felt like a storm, just when I thought I had found some peace.

I remember trying to choke out the words to my mom:

Do I know him? What is his name?

I got a response.

I screamed.

I fell to the ground.

I'm certain the whole neighborhood heard me. The sound was primal, coming from a place deep inside that I didn't even know existed. In that moment, Grace rushed over, nuzzling her face into my leg, grounding me with her presence. She was right there, by my side, reminding me I wasn't alone, even in the midst of this storm.

The answer I had waited seven years for absolutely terrified me: I didn't know him. He was a stranger. A stalker. That realization made my whole body shudder. This was one of those things you think will never happen to you in a million years—something you only see on crime shows or hear about in some distant, crazy news story. But sometimes, the door of darkness knocks, and it's your door.

The idea that a complete stranger could do this to me—could do this to anyone—was terrifying enough. But then it got worse. After the attack in Arizona, I had moved to California to escape that monster, to distance myself from that part of my life. And yet, without knowing it, I had moved to the very same tiny beach town where my rapist lived.

The weight of that realization hit me like a freight train. I had unknowingly moved closer to the darkness I had spent so long trying to escape.

When I lived in Newport Beach, for many years we were on 40th Street. After all this time, when my rapist was finally caught, it turned out he had been apprehended just one block away, on 41st Street, attempting to break into a house where young women lived. While he wasn't living there, I later learned he had been residing in the same county as me all those years.

He was caught trying to break into a home where three women lived. When the police questioned him, he resisted, which in California is a felony. That arrest triggered a process that would change everything. At booking, they took his photographs, his fingerprints, and—most importantly—a DNA sample.

Let me zoom out for a moment and explain something about DNA collection. California is one of just nineteen states in the US that collects DNA upon all felony arrests. In all fifty states, DNA is collected upon felony conviction, but only nineteen collect DNA for every single felony arrest, regardless of the charge. Thirty-one states only collect under certain criteria—like for violent felony arrests or burglary. But in California, they collect for every felony arrest.

I thank God every single day that he was arrested in California.

Because of this, they took a DNA swab from my rapist—a simple saliva sample. When they uploaded that DNA into the Combined DNA Index System (CODIS), it matched the DNA from my rape kit, all those years ago in Arizona.

CODIS, if you're not familiar, is the United States' national DNA database. It's a system that operates local, state, and national databases of DNA profiles from convicted offenders, unsolved crime scene evidence, and even missing persons. Without that system, and without California's law, who knows how much longer he would have stayed out there, hurting more women.

More horrifying news, but not unexpected: my rape kit wasn't the only one that had a match. There were others. Still, my evidence was the strongest, so my case was going to go first.

I was numb as the details ticked through my mind like a broken record, one horrifying fact after another about my attacker.

He was a serial rapist. He had a wife, a young son. He was a stalker. A stranger. When the police arrested him, they found a shed filled with women's underwear and ID cards from all over the world. He had a job. He traveled.

I knew I wasn't the first. Seven years had passed since my rape. I knew I hadn't been the last.

But maybe now he would be stopped. Maybe now he would be caught.

Despite that glimmer of hope, I spiraled. I became fixated on researching everything I could find about this man. It consumed me. I was desperate to make sense of it all, but it was hard—really, really hard. And through it all, I was still keeping this a secret from the outside world. Most people in my life had no idea. My brother, who I'm incredibly close with, still didn't know.

The weight of keeping this locked inside was suffocating. But I wasn't ready to let the world in on my pain.

Not yet.

# 8

# Wanderlust

IN 2010, THE same year my perpetrator was arrested, I went to a huge yoga festival at Lake Tahoe in Squaw Valley. It was set in the middle of the most majestic mountains, with crystal-blue lakes that seemed to reflect the sky's soul. Some of the biggest names in yoga were there. We practiced yoga outdoors all day, went on yoga hikes, and enjoyed concerts under the stars at night, surrounded by beautiful lighting. It was wild for me—holding hands and finding connection with strangers at a time when strangers still terrified me. But something shifted in me. It cracked my heart open, and I could feel the stirrings of transformation deep in my soul. I wanted everyone to experience that kind of profound connection.

When I came home from the festival, I felt inspired to move forward with becoming a certified yoga teacher. During the training, several of us wove feathers into our hair as a symbol of our journey. Over time, everyone else's feathers fell out, but mine held on, almost like it was waiting for something.

One night during training, we focused on releasing our hips. Symbolically, this area of the body is associated with the sacral chakra, where trauma is often stored. Of course, it made perfect sense that my hips had always been the tightest part of my body. As we worked through the poses, I started to gain trust in myself. My confidence grew, and slowly, my hips—normally locked up, rock-hard—began to loosen. And then, in a moment that felt strangely significant, my feather finally fell out of my hair.

It felt like freedom.

The feather falling wasn't just a coincidence—it was symbolic of the trauma I had been carrying, stored inside my body for nearly a decade. It was as if my body was finally letting go of the weight I had been suppressing all those years. For the first time, I started to feel closure.

But even with all this forward momentum, I was still nervous to practice teach. My voice wasn't strong. I didn't feel powerful. When I spoke, I wasn't commanding the room the way I knew I needed to. We had to teach in a circle, with the other trainees and leaders watching, and when I finished, I thought I had done great—only to receive feedback that shook me.

"Your voice isn't strong enough. We could barely hear you at times. You paced around, not wanting to be seen. Your students need to hear you, see you. You have to work on commanding the room."

It was a gut check. But it was exactly what I needed to hear.

My teacher offered some guidance after that tough feedback, and I went home that night and cried. I felt utterly defeated. I had thought teaching yoga was my calling, but maybe I didn't have it in me after all. I let the self-doubt wash over me. But after a good cry, I said a prayer, got some rest, and woke up the next morning with something new: a feeling of strength, power, and resilience.

In the shower, I started reciting my class out loud, imagining the energy I wanted to command, envisioning the room of trainees and teachers hanging on my words. I came back to training with confidence. My voice was strong. I felt powerful. I commanded the room, and it felt good. Really good.

Afterward, my teacher jokingly asked, "What did you have for breakfast?" We laughed, but in that moment, I knew something had shifted.

I thought back to the connection I had experienced at the yoga festival, and I felt a deep calling to create something similar—a space that felt big and magical, like that festival, right here in my hometown of Austin, Texas. A place where people could come together and feel seen, feel connected.

When I graduated from yoga teacher training, I was still working at my dad's advertising agency downtown. I started teaching donation-based classes at Betty Sport. I was improving, yes, but I hadn't told my story. There was still this dark cloud looming over my head, this weight I couldn't fully shake.

Then an opportunity came up to teach yoga through Safe Place, a sanctuary for survivors of domestic violence and sexual violence. Safe Place is in a secure, unmarked location, providing women and children a refuge away from the world. It was deeply impactful for me—both to be there for the women I was serving and for myself.

The first time I taught there, we held class in the emergency trauma area, crammed into a tiny toy closet in the emergency center. I wasn't trained in trauma-informed yoga, but I was trauma-informed. I knew what it felt like to carry that weight, to be in a place of deep hurt. The women in my class had come from dangerous situations.

They were there for healing, just like I had been. I felt ill-equipped in so many ways, but I showed up.

I dimmed the lights. I had my little boombox with me, playing music from Patty Griffin. I played "Let It Be." The music that had been such a huge part of softening my own heart, I now shared with others.

There's a beautiful saying that healers need healing too. In addition to teaching the women at Safe Place, I was also teaching the staff. Every day at 11 a.m., during their lunch break, we held yoga classes. These became some of my favorite moments—to take care of the caretakers, the ones who were holding space for women and families in crisis. It felt meaningful to give back in that way.

My dad always taught me:

You can do what you love, work hard, and make a living. You don't want to be good at what you're bad at. You want to be GREAT at what you're good at.

But at my desk job, I wasn't showing up to my fullest potential. I was being good at what I was bad at. I felt unfulfilled, and I knew that splitting my time between desk work and teaching a few yoga classes wasn't going to cut it. Deep down, I knew I could be great. I was ready to answer the calling that had been building in my heart—to open my own yoga studio with that same sense of wanderlust and magic I had experienced at the yoga festival.

So, after much blood, sweat, and tears, I opened the first Wanderlust studio in April of 2012, in a gorgeous warehouse downtown. The space had high ceilings with poles, a vibrant café, and a sanctuary-like feel—but it didn't start that way.

I took out loans, made a huge investment, and poured my heart into the build-out. But the saying, "If you build it, they will come," was not true for me. No one came.

It was terrifying. I had put so much of myself into this dream, only to find empty mats in an empty studio. The bills kept piling up, and I had to find a way to pay them. It was a hard reality to face, but I wasn't ready to give up.

In those early days, I was teaching fourteen classes a week. I used to joke that I should just bring an air mattress and sleep at the studio. I worked my butt off. I had a business partner at the time, but when that didn't work out, I kept it going on my own. There were days I'd invite the girls working in the café to come take a class, just so it looked like we had students.

I remember one time teaching YoStrong—a yoga class with weights and heat. Except, I didn't have the money to install a proper heating system yet, so we used tiny space heaters from Walmart. Picture this: a giant studio that could hold 300 people, and there we were, three of us in a circle. Two girls I pulled from the café, still wearing their denim shorts, and me. It was such a trip.

I'd set my alarm for 4 a.m., 4:05 a.m., 4:10 a.m.—just to make sure I'd get up in time to arrive early, light the candles, turn on the music, and set the vibe for the 6 a.m. class. I'd pace the studio floor, looking out at the dark, quiet streets of downtown Austin, feeling like the world was still asleep.

I remember standing there, looking at the clock: 5:55 a.m.—no one. 5:56 a.m.—still no one. 5:57 a.m.—nothing. By 6 a.m., I saw a car drive by and thought, *Maybe this is it. Maybe someone's finally coming.* But I watched as the headlights turned and disappeared down another street.

At one point, I even found myself looking out at the homeless people nearby and wondering if I should offer to teach them—just to have someone in the studio, just to keep the momentum going.

The sun rose, and no one came to the 6 a.m. class. I remember standing there, feeling defeated, and I called my dad. I told him, I don't think I can make these payments. His response was simple: You gotta figure it out. Honestly, it was the best advice he ever gave me.

So, I changed gears. I got the best people working at the front desk—people who knew everyone's name, who made everyone feel like they had just walked into their second home. This studio was going to be the "Cheers" of yoga studios, where everybody knows your name. My prayer was that it would be a place of fun, hope, and healing.

By our one-year anniversary in April of 2013, we had packed the back studio room with 110 people, mat to mat. DJs from Thievery Corporation created sacred space with live music while I taught yoga. The leap of faith I had taken in opening the studio was finally paying off—spiritually, emotionally, and physically. Not only were people getting stronger and healthier, but we had created jobs, paid off debts, and built a community that was healing together.

I felt that if even one person found the kind of healing that I had found in Toni's studio back in Newport Beach, it was all worth it.

As the studio grew, so did my family. My husband and I wanted to have a baby, but the journey to get pregnant was harder than we expected. After two intrauterine insemination sessions, I became pregnant with our first child. We were elated. We didn't care about the sex and chose not to find out—we decided on the name Charlie, no matter the gender. We were just so grateful.

In April of 2014, five years into owning the yoga studio, our son Charlie was born. Those first eight months were full of joy and happiness, but a part of me knew that the trial still loomed over me like a dark cloud. Despite all the wonderful blessings in my life, I knew that one day, I would have to face it. I would have to go back.

# 9

# Trial

THERE WERE TWO reasons we had to wait five years for the trial. First, we were waiting on a Supreme Court ruling in *Maryland vs. King (2013)*. The court's decision enacted legislative measures that allowed DNA to be taken through a cheek swab upon qualifying arrests, much like taking fingerprints or photographs. The ruling made it clear that DNA collection was reasonable and just under the Fourth Amendment.

The second reason was far more personal—my perpetrator decided to represent himself. It was a disaster. He prolonged the trial process painfully, dragging it out for years.

Then, in December of 2014, I got a phone call from the prosecuting attorney, Ryan Powell. His voice was steady as he said, "Ashley, there will be no more postponements. The trial is set for May of 2015. It's time."

I hung up the phone, and the excuses started pouring in. My son is so young. It feels unnatural to be separated from him. My yoga business is finally turning a profit, after all the years of struggle, after teaching just two people in a room that could hold 100. My team needs me, my community needs me, my family needs me.

It felt like the trial couldn't have come at a worse time. The timing felt impossible. I didn't think I could just drop everything and leave to deal with it.

But deep down, I knew these were all just excuses. The truth was, I had been avoiding this for years, hiding behind everything else in my life—my business, my family, my responsibilities. I wasn't ready to face it, but I knew I had to.

The truth was, I was absolutely terrified to face him again. This man had once looked me in the eyes and told me that if I ever told anyone, he would kill me. And I had a son. The fear of him hurting me—hurting my family—was overwhelming. I didn't know how to handle it. The entire trial was built solely on DNA evidence from my rape kit, and yet the thought of being in that courtroom with him again made me feel like that terrified girl all over again.

I called Ryan, the prosecutor, and he assured me that the decision to go to trial was entirely mine. He said, "I understand whatever you decide. If you choose not to move forward, the most he'll get is ten years." I sat there in silence, feeling the weight of that decision pressing down on me. It felt like I sat there for two hours, but I was no closer to knowing what to do.

I was trying to carry this decision on my own, not wanting to burden my family and friends. I hadn't even told my parents that the trial date had been set. The shame and embarrassment still lingered, even after all these years. My husband knew what had happened to me, but we never talked about it. It was like this shadow hanging over us, always present, but never acknowledged.

Days passed. I kept trying to push the decision away, going through the motions of daily life—getting up, feeding my son, taking him to daycare, teaching yoga. Then one day, I started feeling symptoms that made me think I needed to see my gynecologist. I figured it was probably cysts again or something related to my irregular periods. Before scheduling the appointment, they suggested I take a pregnancy test. I laughed at the thought, but I went ahead and took it at home, fully expecting it to be negative. I left the test on the back of the toilet and didn't even look at it—I was that certain I wasn't pregnant.

Later that day, I came home, glanced at the test, and there it was—a positive sign. I was shocked. I called my husband, and he was just as surprised as I was. Our kids were going to be just eighteen months apart.

I confided in my parents that our family was growing once again, and that they would have another grandchild by October of 2015. Of course, they were elated and supportive, as they always were.

I was even less sure about going to trial now that I was pregnant again. The idea of going through that process while carrying a child felt overwhelming. Since we hadn't found out the gender with Charlie, we decided to find out this time. I'll never forget the moment we got the letter from the doctor's office. It said, You're having a baby girl. Chills swept over my entire body, and tears filled my eyes.

In that instant, everything became clear. Not going to trial was no longer an option. I told myself: Ashley, you ARE going to trial—not just for yourself, but for your daughter, for everyone's daughter, everyone's sister, everyone's friend. You're going.

That was it. I picked up the phone, called the prosecutor, and said, "Let's do this. Let's go to trial."

I was scared to tell my dad. The thought of facing the rapist in court with his granddaughter in my belly terrified me. But I knew what I had to do. I got online, booked a flight to Phoenix, and prepared myself for what was ahead. Then I drove over to my parents' house, my one-year-old son in the backseat, and dropped him off.

Without much warning, I told them I was flying out that day to go to the trial. I'll never forget the look on my mom's face—her complexion drained as she swept my son up into her arms and carried him into the other room. My dad, always steady, walked me outside to my car. He looked at me and asked what I was talking about.

I told him the truth, "Dad, this is something I have to do."

His face softened, and with a depth that only he could offer, he looked me in the eyes and said, "Godspeed, daughter."

Getting on the plane to Phoenix was one of the hardest, most surreal moments of my life. Although my husband and I ultimately separated, he supported me through this. He went with me to the trial. I'm forever grateful to him. In the face of unimaginable darkness, he stood by me.

The man who had violently raped me and threatened to kill me if I ever told anyone was now standing in front of me—live, in full color—representing himself and calling me a liar, right to my face. It was like stepping into a nightmare. He made his own opening statements. He questioned me. I sat there in shock as he accused me of stalking him, of following him to Newport Beach and eating at the same restaurants where he was.

I couldn't take it. I screamed in panic and ran out of the courtroom, unable to breathe.

Look for the light.

That day, Rhonda was my light. She was a victim advocate, and her job was to hold hands, wipe tears, and make a stranger—in this case, me—feel less alone in the storm. She followed me outside the courtroom, where I collapsed on the floor. "He's not telling the truth!" I sobbed to her, my body curled up in a fetal position, completely overwhelmed.

Rhonda knelt beside me, gently rubbing my back. She spoke softly, "Ashley, he's lying. Breathe. It's okay. He's lying. Just breathe."

I couldn't comprehend what was happening. The lies. The audacity. I was being forced to relive it all—the 911 calls, the photographs, every tear, every horrible thing that had happened. Fear and anger surged through me. It was like being trapped in a nightmare I couldn't escape.

# Trial

When it was my turn to testify, he must've realized how out of his depth he was because suddenly, a defense attorney appeared. When they called my name, I walked through the door, and there he was. I had to walk past the man who had violated every part of my being. I could feel my skin harden on the left side of my body, like armor trying to protect me. I looked at the judge, then at the jury, and for a moment, I almost ran out of the room again. Every instinct in me screamed to flee. But I planted my feet, took a deep breath, and told myself, You have to do this.

With my legs shaking and every ounce of courage I had, I stood my ground. I was there to tell my story.

I have such deep empathy for every woman who has to walk into that courtroom, who has to face that kind of fear.

I'll never forget taking my seat. My body trembled as I held up my hand to take the oath, swearing to tell the truth. The weight of every eye in that courtroom was on me. I rested my hand on my pregnant belly and felt strength pour through me from my daughter. My heart shattered into a thousand pieces as the defense attorney stood up and began his questioning.

He tried to pick apart my story, to find cracks in my truth. He accused me of meeting this monster in a cab and suggested we had consensual relations, questioning how the DNA ended up on my chest. He questioned my integrity, my sexual history, and my honesty. He was defending a man who had broken into my home, raped me in my own bed, and nearly killed me, and yet there he was, lying for him.

I felt rage take over my body.

But rage—rage became my superpower.

By the time the prosecutor stood up to ask his questions, I was no longer afraid. I felt the wrath of God surging through my veins. I spoke with fierce honesty. I spoke with bravery. I spoke with courage. The words of a quote echoed in my mind: "The human spirit is stronger than anything that can happen to it." And in that moment, I felt the truth of those words in my bones.

My spirit was on fire, fueled by the strength of the tiny baby girl growing inside of me.

The trial was filled with so much darkness. I was forced to face this monster—no pillow to block my vision this time, just his eyes locked on mine, only feet away. I had to relive the 911 calls, look at every photograph of terror, abuse, and violence, and be reminded of every single horrific detail. It felt like an out-of-body experience, as if I was watching it all unfold as the main character in some tragic movie. "This cannot be my life," I kept thinking.

But even in the midst of all that darkness, there was light. My dad had always taught me to look for it, and in those moments, I did. It surrounded me in ways I hadn't expected.

The light was in Officer Williams, the first police officer who had responded the night of the attack. He was incredibly tall, and as I stood outside the courtroom, he leaned down, wrapped me in a warm hug, and said, "I remember you. Wow! I'm so proud of the young woman you've become!" His words were a lifeline, grounding me in the present.

The light was in Jennifer, my forensic nurse. She flew all the way to Phoenix from San Antonio to testify. After thirteen years, she still remembered me—she remembered my case. I couldn't believe it. She had helped thousands of survivors over the span of her career, yet she held space for me, flying across the country to stand by my side.

The light was in the detectives, Detective Gentry and Detective Bailey, who never gave up hope, even when I did. One of them showed me a picture—one taken the very night my life was shattered, a photo of me and my friends inside my apartment. He told me he taped that picture to his computer and looked at it every single day. It wasn't just a reminder of what happened to me; it was a reminder of what could happen to his own daughter. He saw everyone's daughter in that photo, and that's why he kept fighting for answers, every single day.

The light was in the prosecutor, Ryan Powell, who worked tirelessly, day and night, to make sure this man would never be free to harm another person again.

The light was in the DNA analysts. Before the trial, I knew nothing about forensic DNA. I was a yoga girl, an entrepreneur. Forensic science and the incredible work done by crime labs was a world I never imagined I'd rely on. But the trial hinged on DNA evidence and DNA legislation. I had never seen this man's face. I couldn't have picked him out of a lineup. He was a stranger, a stalker. Yet here we were, all because of DNA—because someone fought to make sure that justice could be served, even when it felt impossible.

The DNA analysts in my case did their job with such precision and care that they were able to prove it was 38 trillion times more likely that this man's DNA was on me than anyone else's. Thirty-eight trillion. In 2010, they used an advanced DNA testing method called YSTR, which allowed them to separate the X chromosome from the Y chromosome. When they did that, they found his DNA all over my body. And even more compelling? The DNA aligned perfectly with every story of abuse, rape, and attack that I had told detectives right after my assault.

This made the evidence in court clear, undeniable. DNA is science, and DNA is truth. I never wanted the wrong person to serve time for this horrific crime, and that evidence—the science—gave me, and the jury, peace of mind.

All of the people I've mentioned, they are truly my angels. I believe they were put on this earth by a higher power, to help me—and countless others—get through. Without each of them working together, I honestly don't know if I'd still be here today. I am certain that without forensic DNA, without advanced testing methods, or with outdated collection laws, this man would still be out there today, free to rape and harm other women.

I flew back home, but the trial continued. I wanted to get back to my son, to my daughter growing inside me. Being in the studio, teaching yoga, helped me feel some sense of normalcy. It was grounding.

But still, I hadn't shared with anyone at work, or even my own brother, that I had been flying back and forth to Phoenix to attend the trial for a home invasion rape that I had barely survived in college. It was a deep, dark secret that I kept buried inside.

A few weeks passed, and I focused my energy on staying in the present—on my family, on my work. The trial felt like a distant memory, like an episode from a Netflix show. It didn't feel real. I couldn't connect it to my own life. In my heart, I believe our bodies and minds have a way of disconnecting from overwhelming situations to help us survive the pain. So, I went about my normal life, doing what I had to do—surviving. I was growing a child in my belly, focusing on the future.

Then, I got the call.

I was walking in downtown Austin on my way to teach a yoga class. It was sweltering hot—summer in Texas. Ryan and Rhonda were on the other end of the line, and before they even said a word, I could hear it in their voices. Ashley—he's guilty.

Tears immediately welled up in my eyes. I started sobbing—deep, uncontrollable sobs. He's guilty.

A student who had been coming to the studio for years saw me crying and came over, concerned. My tears were flowing, and I was a mess. She looked into my eyes and asked if I was okay. I nodded, barely able to whisper, "I'm okay. I'm okay." I hadn't told anyone at the studio about what had happened to me—not about the rape, not about the trial, and not even about my pregnancy.

She went inside, and I wiped my tears, pulled myself together as best I could, and walked into the studio to teach a room full of eighty yogis.

But in my heart, I still couldn't believe it.

*He's guilty.*

In October of 2015, just a few months after the trial, my precious daughter was born. I always knew she would be strong. She not only carried me through the trial, but I know her soul must have absorbed some of that difficult energy. Growing up, my mom always loved the movie *Gone with the Wind*. Whenever I'd have a tough day, she'd remind me of the main character, Scarlett, and her strength. Scarlett would say, "I can't think about that right now. If I do, I'll go crazy. I'll think about that tomorrow."

My mom raised me with that mindset. Don't focus on the hard times. Be strong. Be brave. Don't feel it. You'll get through. And, in many ways, that mindset did help me survive. It got me through some of the hardest moments of my life.

But as I've walked my own healing journey, I've learned that feeling is crucial—having a voice, speaking up, being heard—that's what heals. Still, I want to pause and honor the generations that came before us. They may not have been able to process emotions in the healthiest way, but they were undeniably strong. And there's something powerful in that.

Scarlett O'Hara was fiercely strong, and I knew my daughter would be too. That's why I named her Scarlett. She even had reddish hair when she was born, though it didn't last.

Yoga gave me the gift of being present—of "be here now." And that practice became my lifeline. I had to be present every hour, every day, while we waited for sentencing. An entire year passed before sentencing began.

In May of 2016, it was time to fly back to Phoenix for sentencing. Once again, my parents watched my kids, and my husband came with me. The entire experience felt surreal—like watching a crime show, except this was my life. It was as if I had become a character in an unimaginable true crime movie. I was nervous, angry, relieved—all at once. Nothing felt good.

Before going into the courtroom, Ryan, the prosecuting attorney, pulled me aside. "I want you to know this man's family is here," he said.

Family? I gasped. My heart sank. Having a family humanized him. It was gut-wrenching. I didn't want to think of him as a "normal" person, as a husband, or as a father. I wanted to believe he was a monster, not someone with a family who loved him.

Ryan quickly corrected me. "No, no, no—they're here in support of you. They've flown here from all over to be here for you. They want to know if they can speak with you."

I nodded, completely in disbelief. We approached each other, solemnly at first, and then we cried. I hugged his niece, his nephew, and his sister. We all apologized to each other, our souls connected in shared despair. We were all devastated by the ripple effects of his violence. The devastation didn't end with me—it spread out to everyone connected to him.

His family wasn't the only group there in support. A painter, someone who had grown up with the perpetrator, had driven hours to "watch him fry." This man had an extensive history of getting into trouble.

During sentencing, his sister asked to speak to the judge. I sat in the courtroom, my nerves raw, and watched as she walked up to the microphone. The back of her blonde hair was facing me as she began to speak. I felt a heavy wave of despair, empathy, and sadness wash over me. I couldn't imagine the courage it took to stand there, facing her own brother, and say what she did.

Her words held truth. They held power. "I'm a detective in my own life because I had to grow up with him as a brother. We are certain he has killed people, and I am asking you today—never let my brother see the light of day again. He should never see the light of day again."

The courtroom was thick with shock and emotion. It was so quiet, you could hear a pin drop. Silence blanketed the room as we all waited for the verdict. The jury had deliberated for less than an hour when the judge finally spoke. From the back of the courtroom, I heard the words that would change everything: "You're sentenced to 137.5 years in prison." My head fell into my hands as the tears poured out. I cried and cried. He was sentenced to the maximum time allowed in Arizona.

I was free.

But with that freedom came a storm of emotions. Tragedy. Freedom. I was fortunate to have justice. And yet, I couldn't help but think—every victim deserves this.

I knew, at that moment, I couldn't stay silent anymore.

Yes, there was relief in knowing he would be locked away for the entirety of his life, my life, and my children's lives. But with that relief came a profound questioning of my spirituality. Everything does NOT happen for a reason. I had been born and raised Catholic, but I couldn't believe in a God who would allow this to happen to me—or to anyone else, for that matter. The spiritual teachings I had grown up with no longer made sense. I had spent the last decade in deep pain, and now, without an ounce of faith.

After the trial, I started sharing my story with a few select women I had known for years. What shocked me—what horrified me—was that seven out of the eight of them had a similar story. Seven out of eight. How could this be? And how could we all have been living in silence for so long?

Throughout the trial process, I had watched other people—parents who had lost their daughters in situations like mine, but with an even worse ending. Their daughters were brutally raped and murdered. And these parents, in the face of that unimaginable loss, would forgive the murderer because of their faith. I couldn't make sense of that. Forgiveness didn't feel possible to me. It didn't make sense.

I couldn't understand how so much violence and cruelty wasn't being discussed. And when it was discussed, how quickly people seemed to turn to forgiveness. I may have won the trial, but in that process, I lost my faith. However, anything lost can be found again, and ultimately, I would find a deeper and unshakable faith that sustains me to this day.

# 10

# Forgiveness and Healing

AFTER THE TRIAL ended, I craved something to heal the deep, raw wound that had been left behind. So, I found myself at a Wanderlust Festival in Colorado, drawn by the promise of renewal. I signed up for a class taught by M.C. Yogi and his wife. These two weren't just yoga instructors—they were storytellers, musicians, weavers of wisdom. I couldn't have predicted this beforehand, but the class was a blend of everything I needed: music, chanting, movement, and stories about letting go, surrendering, forgiveness, and freeing yourself.

It felt like a journey, one where the stories they shared wound their way through each pose we held, speaking directly to the parts of me that needed to heal. By the end, my body was drenched in sweat, my muscles shaking from exertion, but something more profound was happening within me.

As we sat quietly, meditating on our mats, they handed each of us a small piece of paper and a pen. I stared at the blank page, unsure of what to expect. "Write down something you're ready to let go of," they said, their voices gentle yet firm. It was an invitation, a challenge, really—to confront what I had been holding onto for far too long. Then, we were instructed to place that piece of paper in a prayer wheel, a large, vintage-looking cylinder that had traveled the world with them. It was covered in red graffiti-like writing, symbols of release. You wrote, placed your paper inside, gave it a spin, and let go.

I sat there, pen poised above the paper, and had no idea what I was going to write. Then, as if a dam broke inside me, the words came, and they were as much a shock to me as they were a revelation. Tears began to stream down my cheeks as I scrawled, "Kevin Lee Francois, I forgive you."

The words felt foreign, almost absurd. Forgiveness? I had told myself over and over that I would never forgive. I didn't even want to forgive. I used to watch families on the news—families whose children had been taken from them in horrific ways—and when they would say they forgave the person responsible, I couldn't fathom it. How could you ever forgive such a monster?

But I remembered something Jeff Krasno, one of Wanderlust's founders, had said on a podcast I once did

## Forgiveness and Healing

with him. He told me that holding on to anger was like holding on to a hot ember—it only burns you. I didn't want to keep holding that ember anymore.

As I wrote those words—words I had never expected to write—my hand trembled. My tears fell silently as I made my way to the prayer wheel, the sound of chanting and soft singing filling the room. It was as though the energy of the space was lifting me, guiding me toward this moment of release. I dropped my small piece of paper inside the prayer wheel, gave it a spin, and stood there, feeling the weight I had carried for thirteen long years begin to shift.

When I sat back down on my mat, the tears came again, but this time they felt different. Lighter, somehow. Something in me had shifted. I'll never forget walking out of that room, the feeling of the Colorado mountains surrounding me, the air crisp with possibility. I pushed open the double doors with both hands, letting the bright sun pour onto my face, my heart, my spirit. And in that moment, as I stood there with my arms spread wide, I felt it—freedom.

I took a deep breath and thought, *I am finally free.*

Forgiveness is never easy. It's messy, unpredictable, and requires more strength than I ever thought I had.

There's no step-by-step guide for it, no timetable, no right or wrong way to do it. For me, it took years of holding onto anger, pain, and grief before I was ready to let it go. But when I did, I found something I had been searching for all along—the key to my own healing. The greatest piece of my journey was forgiveness, and I hadn't even known it was missing until that moment.

Healing, I've learned, is a process. It's not linear, and it's never simple. But forgiveness? Forgiveness was my way forward. It was my way to reclaim the parts of myself that I had lost along the way. In that moment of release, I realized: I wasn't just letting go of the past. I was letting go of everything that had been holding me back.

But at the end of the day, forgiveness is really about something bigger than itself. Forgiveness, if it's genuine, brings healing. Letting go of the pain opens us up to a future untethered from the pain of our past.

Healing is not a straight line. It's not a step-by-step guide with neat instructions or a destination you reach and then move on. Healing is messy, difficult, and painful, yet on the other side, it's so raw, gorgeous, and beautifully human. It shows us what it really means to be alive. I've come to understand this truth through my own journey—a truth that is as freeing as it is terrifying.

## Forgiveness and Healing

One of my teachers, Dan Nevins from the Wounded Warrior Project, always says, "In order to heal, you have to feel." Those words have been my mantra, my anchor. They mean feeling everything—the life-shattering pain, the unbridled joy, the awkward messiness, and the moments of deep connection. It's all part of the process, and there's no skipping over it. No fast-forward button. You have to sit in the discomfort, let yourself be vulnerable, and feel it all.

It's tempting to get lost in the false narratives that surround us—the glossy perfectionism of social media, the pressure to "have it all together." But the truth is, life is messy. Healing is messy. And when we stop pretending, when we boldly and vulnerably own that messiness, something incredible happens. Our lives begin to change in ways we never imagined. It's not just our lives that change—it's the lives of the people around us, too. When we show up as our real, unpolished selves, we give others permission to do the same. And that, my friends, is where real healing begins.

I remember one day during my own healing journey, I felt an overwhelming urge to find a new tattoo. I wanted something that would remind me of this process—something that would symbolize not just the destination but the journey itself. As I searched, I came across the most beautiful depiction of a Greek goddess named Akeso. I was instantly drawn to her. Akeso symbolizes the process of healing, not the cure. How poignant is that? She wasn't the goddess of a quick fix or a neat resolution. She was the embodiment of the journey, the continual process of healing.

At that moment, I realized, she is me. She is all of us. Akeso represents the truth of what it means to heal—that it's a lifelong journey. Healing isn't something we check off a to-do list and then move on from. It's something we live, day in and day out. It's time to own it, to live it, to be it, to embrace the process fully.

Healing doesn't mean you'll never feel pain again. It doesn't mean you'll be "fixed" or "perfect." But it does mean that you are alive, that you are growing, that you are fully embracing the beauty of your own resilience. It's about honoring every part of yourself—the messy, the beautiful, the painful, and the joyful. Because when you do that, you begin to understand what it truly means to heal. You begin to understand what it means to feel.

The truth is, healing will ask everything of you. It will ask you to let go of who you thought you needed to be and embrace who you truly are. That's a gift. Because when we embrace the process, when we accept that healing isn't a destination but a lifelong journey, we find a kind of peace that isn't reliant on external circumstances. We find a peace that comes from within.

So, here's to Akeso. Here's to the process, the journey, the mess, and the beauty. Healing is not a linear path, but it's ours to walk. As we walk it, we become more alive, more compassionate, and more connected to our truest selves.

# Epilogue

WORKING IN POLITICS is not for the faint of heart. When I founded the DNA Justice Project, I thought, *this mission is so powerful, so obvious, that anyone who hears our story will be on board.* I believed that passing laws to save lives and exonerate the innocent would be a no-brainer—people would see it, feel it, and fight for it. But what I quickly learned is that making change, real systemic change, is hard. And, as frustrating as that can be, it's also necessary. It's one of the most vulnerable and challenging things I've ever done.

I've had to learn how to navigate a world that isn't always welcoming. Booking flights at the last minute, leaving behind the life I know as a mother, has become routine. It's hard, so hard, but I'm lucky to have a supportive family and a co-parent who's active in our child's life, making it all possible. Even so, it's a grind. I've flown across the country to advocate for our mission, often on a shoestring budget, staying in roadside hotels. There's nothing glamorous about it—just me, alone, often feeling isolated. Yet, what keeps me going is the belief that this work matters.

There's a quote by Dr. Wayne Dyer that I carry with me like a shield: *"If you knew who walked beside you on the path that you have chosen, you would never experience fear or doubt again."* I think of that often when I find myself arriving at some unfamiliar capitol building, late at night, tired but determined. The next morning, I'm knocking on the doors of senators, representatives, delegates—whoever will listen. And I have two minutes, maybe less, to tell my story, to convince them that DNA policies are essential for saving lives, delivering justice, and exonerating the innocent. It's raw, it's vulnerable, and often, it's awkward.

I've become somewhat of a detective myself, researching every politician I'm about to meet. I dig into their voting history, their committee memberships, even their personal lives. Do they have daughters? Would this issue resonate with them on a personal level? Despite all the research, I'm often blindsided by who ends up supporting the bill—and who doesn't.

I remember one meeting in Arizona vividly. I was nervous about it. The man I was about to meet was a staunch civil libertarian, and I thought for sure he

## Epilogue

would oppose us. My heart pounded as I shared my story. Alongside me was Jayann Sepich, who had lost her daughter, Katie Sepich, to violence. As we spoke, I saw something shift in him—his eyes welled up with tears behind his glasses. He told us he had once been a police officer and had seen firsthand the aftermath of brutal assaults. He hugged us and said, "I will do everything in my power to make this law pass."

Moments like that remind me why I do this. It's not easy—far from it. The process of passing a bill is grueling. Meetings, testimonies, hearings, votes—it's a marathon that you repeat again and again, often ending in disappointment. Arizona, for example, felt like fate. I was sure the law would pass there, but at the last minute, it fell apart. After months of hard work, it failed spectacularly. The backlash was fierce, with some arguing that DNA collection infringed on their rights. I was devastated. I felt like I had been gutted, left empty after pouring so much of my heart into the fight.

The work isn't just physically exhausting, with flights and long days on your feet—it's emotionally draining. You open yourself up, telling your story over and over, knowing that it could save lives, and still, you're met with opposition. It's like laying your heart on the table, only to watch it get shattered.

But as my dad taught me, there's light, even in the darkest moments. In West Virginia, after pouring my heart out to a representative I thought would support us, I was met with coldness, even condescension. I left that meeting feeling defeated, barely holding back tears. I cried in the bathroom for what felt like hours before pulling myself together. I had to testify in front of the judiciary committee later that day, and the same woman was on the committee. I was shaking, but I prayed. I asked God to make me a conduit for this truth, to help me deliver this message with grace and strength. And though she voted against it, the others voted for it. We didn't win, but I found peace in knowing that I was fighting for what was right.

One of the hardest lessons I've learned is that it's not always about the outcome. Sometimes, the real victory is in showing up, in speaking your truth even when it feels impossible. I think about my friend James Tillman, who was exonerated through DNA evidence after spending years in prison for a rape he didn't commit. He's a testament to why this fight matters—to why we can't stop, no matter how many doors close.

# Epilogue

Then, there are the moments of triumph. In my home state of Texas, after years of hard work, we passed a law that made Texas the nineteenth state to collect DNA upon felony arrest. I'll never forget the feeling of walking into the Senate chamber with my children, seeing the law pass unanimously. It was a moment I had worked for, cried for, fought for. The first year after the law passed, over 260 cold cases were solved. That's what keeps me going—the knowledge that this work is saving lives.

As I look at my children, I tell them, "Mommy is fighting to protect you, and others, from the kind of pain she went through." They don't know the full story yet, but they know enough. And they know that no matter how hard things get, there's always hope. That's the light I hold onto—turning tragedy into change, turning pain into hope.

This is what the DNA Justice Project stands for. This is what I stand for. For that, I am so grateful.

# Afterword

# Sexual Healing

AT 19 YEARS old, the violent sexual assault I endured stripped away my softness, femininity, trust in men, and sensuality. It took me many years to rebuild that connection. For a long time, I felt a deep-seated hatred for my body, feeling repulsive, foreign in my own skin, and terrified of vulnerability. I have come to understand that sacred and intimate connections with a loving partner are rooted in the ability to be vulnerable.

Following the end of my marriage, I found myself in tumultuous and sometimes abusive relationships. However, I eventually recognized that the core of my relationship struggles was not from my partners, but from a lack of self-love within me. I reached a low point, unsure of how to love myself, but during my healing journey, I discovered herbal medicine and cooking. This exploration unexpectedly became a pathway to healing both my body and my sensuality. I began preparing fresh meals infused with nourishing seasonal herbs, creating medicinal dishes, and healing elixirs straight from nature. Through this process, I cultivated a profound sense of self-love for my body, mind, spirit, and soul. This transformation shifted the nature of the relationships I attracted as I finally embraced the sacredness of my body.

I am now engaged to a wonderful, strong, and loving man who treats me with tenderness and is incredibly patient as I continue to sensually heal myself in this sacred way. Once I learned to love myself, I was able to build a trusting and beautiful relationship. Our relationship is not without its challenges; it can be messy and difficult at times, but that is the reality of love.

Trevor provides me with a sense of protection, and I always feel safe with him. Sacred intimacy with a partner is a beautiful experience filled with love, trust, and connection. It is one of the most significant aspects of our lives. Although I was never informed of this during my healing process, I hope you see that a connection to healthy, sacred intimacy with a loving partner is possible. No matter where you have come from.